MYSTICAL LIGHTS
A COLLECTION OF POEMS

BY
MANIVASAGAN MOODLEY

To Terry

Wish you all the best on your journey!
& and thank you for your help on my journey!

Take care
Mani Moodley
CGC, 2018

Copyright © 2014 Manivasagan Moodley

Please visit:
www.mysticallights.org

All rights reserved, including the right to reproduce this book, or portions thereof in any form. No part of this text may be reproduced, transmitted, downloaded, decompiled, reverse engineered, or stored, in any form or introduced into any information storage and retrieval system, in any form or by any means, whether electronic or mechanical without the express written permission of the author.

ISBN: 978-1-326-11898-3

Cover artwork by Manivasagan Moodley
Cover design by Scott Gaunt

PublishNation, London
www.publishnation.co.uk

Contents

1. Dedication and Acknowledgements
2. Introduction   1
3. Themes: 3

   a. Through The Dragon's Mind
   b. Earth Light Shine
   c. Eternal Ecstasy
   d. A Walk Through My World
   e. Challenge for Change
   f. One True Light

4. Introductory poem   4
   - Dedicated to Lord Ganesha, the remover of all obstacles

5. Where it all began…   6

   a. Rhythmical Energy Beams   7
   b. Mystical Magical Dragon   8

6. Through the Dragon's Mind   9

   a. The Magician's Story   10
   b. Confessions   11
   c. Dragon Light   12
   d. Unloved Grace   13
   e. Dark Dawn   15
   f. Badge of Love   17
   g. The Witch's Curse   19
   h. Ether   21
   i. Breakfast in Eternity   22

7. Earth Light Shine   23

       a. Freedom   24
       b. The Broken Mirror   25

8. Eternal Ecstasy   27

       a. Another World   28
       b. Stars   29
       c. Halo Infinity   30
       d. One   31
       e. Eternal Ecstasy   33
       f. Existence   35

9. A Walk Through My World   36

       a. A Poet's Solace   37
       b. The Drive   38
       c. Dining With Rats   39
       d. Strings of Heaven   40
       e. Exploration   42
       f. Rented, Unmade Bed   43
       g. True Love Dipped In Blue 44
       h. Juxtaposition   45
       i. Sacred Time   46
       j. The Rescue   48
       k. Internal   49

10.	Challenge for Change		50
	a. Divine Wealth		51
	b. Only God Knows		52
	c. Treasured Gold		54
	d. The Fallen's Immortality		56
11.	One True Light		58
	a. Vibrations		59
	b. Lucid Mind		60
	c. Unborn		62
	d. Echoes of Light		64
	e. Perfect		66
	f. The Return		67
12.	Until We Meet Again		68
13.	About The Poet		69

Dedication

To my late father:
- I miss you. I love you and thank you for everything that you have taught me, the most important thing being honesty.

To my mother Kamala:
- I love you. Thank you for all your love, blessings, and guidance. Your courage, strength and faith have always been inspiring.

To my sister Sujatha:
- You are an amazing soul and I am glad to be a part of your life. Thank you for always believing in me.

Acknowledgements

I am deeply thankful to my sister Sujatha, mother Kamala, and dear friends Chetna, Vina, and Pat for their early reviewing of the manuscript and helpful feedback. Your collective advice, support and guidance are greatly appreciated.

I wish to thank the editorial team at PublishNation for the professional editing of this book. You have done an amazing job.

I further extend gratitude to my friend Roshan for assisting with the layout of the manuscript and IT support.

I also wish to thank all my family and friends who have, over the last few years, supported and encouraged me to have my poems published.

And a final thank you goes to my friend Roy, who helped me in understanding, analysing and appreciating poetry.

Introduction

Poetry is the best way for me to express myself. It gives me freedom to fly to worlds known and unknown. It gives me freedom to stay at home. Writing is my solace and allows me to escape to serenity.

I write in response to my environment, elements, and energy around me.
In the world today,
There is anger and fear and, in the same space and time, love and light.
In the world today,
There is pain and death and, in the same space and time, healing and birth.
In the world today,
There is anxiety and destruction, and also peace and creation.
So I write what I see – what I hear and what I feel.

As I embark on this, my first book of poetry, I feel - firstly - blessed to have this craft and – secondly - excited to have finally completed it.

Some of my poems are written from direct experience and are very personal to me, as these experiences have created and moulded my existence and my reality.

Some of the poems are entangled in altered realities, some in pure sweet fantasy, and some a mixture of both.

This book has taken me a few years to write and it has been a beautiful and interesting journey.

I am now proud to have these experiences published.

Themes

As I reflected upon my poems, it was clear that a few themes were emerging.

1. ***Through the Dragon's Mind:***
   These poems were written when I was swimming in the rainbow of my creative imagination. These are my expressions on reality, fantasy – and everything above, below, and in between. This is probably the best way to describe this section.

2. ***Earth Light Shine:***
   Poems reflecting Mother Earth

3. ***Eternal Ecstasy:***
   Poems dedicated to true love

4. ***A Walk Through My World:***
   Most of these poems are written as a result of personal experience.

5. ***Challenge for Change:***
   Political expressions

6. ***One True Light:***
   Poems on spirituality

INTRODUCTORY POEM

Marching Elephants*

Elephants marching through the jungles of our mind,
Trampling, through the uncertainty,
Stamping down on the ground.

Removing all the unwanted,
Removing the unknown,
Removing the unseen.

Clearing the path.
Pushing forward.
Moving upwards.

God's bliss,
God's grace,
God bless the marching elephants.

Introductory poem, dedicated to Lord Ganesha who, in Hinduism, is the remover of all obstacles.

WHERE IT ALL BEGAN...

Rhythmical Energy Beams

Have you ever seen an angel dance?
Golden wings fluttering in the warm breeze.
Aorta, artery, and vein pumping red thick life
To the beat of the rhythm of the shining light.
Energy now flows.
Angel light spreads throughout the atmosphere
Touching all, everywhere.
Can you feel the magical angel dust
Soft like snow
With its enhancing glow?
You can feel the pulsating motions.
You can smell the angelic presence.
You can visualize it. It is like a dream.
Lucid, serene images now surround you.
A feeling of ecstasy.
No. Something better …
It's the dance of the angels.

Mystical Magical Dragon

Angel light shining bright in my eyes,
Lighting my soul warm within
Igniting the spirit of the magical dragon.

Surges of energy pulsate through my blood, bone, and nerves,
Producing a rainbow of radiant, healing rays,
Removing the insulation from my mind.

I am now becoming free.
Seeing faces in their truest form,
Seeing Mother Nature's expanded beauty.

Mystical, magical dragon fully erupted, flying high,
Heavenly choirs of angels trumpet in glory,
My eyes awash with tears of joy.

My spiritual journey now begins,
The magical dragon's energy vibrates through me,
Enhancing my mind with creativity.

With the mystical dragon illuminating my crown,
And my mind's energy in unlimited expansion,
I bathe in a fountain of golden ecstasy.

THROUGH THE DRAGON'S MIND

1. The Magician's Story
2. Confessions
3. Dragon Light
4. Unloved Grace
5. Dark Dawn
6. Badge of Love
7. The Witch's Curse
8. Ether
9. Breakfast in Eternity

The Magician's Story

Secret gardens run though my mind,
Lost, but known to the magician's hand.
Enchantment draws the crowds in,
All in search of that shiny amulet.

The magic stick laced with poison,
From it dripping blood like resin.
The code of life now on the floor,
Escaping away through the glass door.

Merlin's magic of untold glory,
Seems to be part of the world's ongoing story.
Answers to the ancient questions.
Death deepens the mystery.

As I grasp to understand all this encryption,
Swirling, twirling magic threads run deep.
Awaken me from the witch's sleep,
Bright eyes open wide and clear.

The rainbow awake in full glory,
Now I see the magician's story.
Told in sunlight heavenly words,
The question remains …

Is it a dream?

Confessions

Standing in the light, she dances all night.
She makes no excuses for her tired, worn-out eyes.
She knows she has made mistakes.
She knows only God can judge her.

The stained pavement with the lone street light
Is the platform for her expression:
The stage for her confession.
She has to let this secret out.

She has held this burden for many years.
She has borne the secret as it tore her soul.
Did she make a mistake?
Or was this simply fate?

On that cold December night,
Under that iconic London light.
Did she meet her destiny?
Or was this pure fantasy?

Through the passage of time,
With the knowledge of this crime,
Would she change the course of her history?
Or indulge in the pleasures of mystery?

Dragon Light

Dragon fires burning on the souls of the brave
Escape to the land of the heroes,
Standing tall on the mountains of prophets.
Sing your song, Dragon Light.

As we escape the darkness of the night
They run and hide from all that glitters-
The trivial toys of a modern existence.
Listen to your heart, Dragon Light.

Surrounded by echoes of the past,
Flying around skies of grey,
Silver shards cutting through my face.
Heal your wounds, Dragon Light.

Enveloped in the sarcasm of the world,
Feelings of grime bind in your mind.
Twisted symbols of unreal gods.
Have faith, Dragon Light.

As the world ends, it also begins.
As the song finishes, the silence begins.
The point of no return
Is to return to the point of one.

Journey away into the world of light,
Where snow-white doves fly above.
Rest in bliss. Listen to the angels.
You are home, Dragon Light.

Unloved Grace

The painter stands alone in a room of colour.
His soul is black, his mind is white.
He is all alone
On this cold November night.

He picks up his brush
And wipes away the tears
That now stain his face.
He knows he has lost his place.

She went away, far into space.
He cannot find her.
Even if he did ...
Would he recognise her?

He remembers her voice.
He knew he had to make a choice.
He remembers her scent.
He felt she was heaven-sent.

But decisions have to be made by the brave.
He knew he would have to sacrifice.
He would have to pay the price.
He would bear the duty. He would do right.

So he let her go.
Slip away into the night.
That beautiful bright light
Now faded away.

Was it a worthy sacrifice
To remain alone in a palace of gold?
To feel icy cold
In a room of burning fire.

Destiny had painted his picture.
A tortured, beautiful, serene creature.
He smiled and beamed radiance.
His head dipped in unloved grace.

Dark Dawn

The hunter searches for the prey,
His blood flowing with rage.
He needs to kill.
He relishes the thrill.

The song of the swan
Echoes in his mind.
But he cannot understand
This melody of ancient time.

Why should he be reminded of angels
As he prepares to take a life?
He is not one of God's men.
He is alone on this path.

Devoid of soul and consciousness,
Destroyed by past experience.
God did not listen.
God did not hear his cry.

So why should the light strike now?
He prefers the darkness of light.
Shadows dwell in his mind.
He belongs to the unreal.

Fires rage in his soul,
Light blinding the windows of his mind.
Whispers slowly seep through.
Maybe he can change…

The beast moves away.
He needs to make a decision fast.
Slumber in the dark,
Or reach to the dawn.

Badge of Love

Every Saturday afternoon, just after three,
He stands there,
Alone in the square.
His only desire is to share.

People gather around him,
All hoping to forget.
Hoping to escape
Their worries and regrets.

Always the same hat.
Always the same shirt.
Always the blue jeans.
And always the smile.

This is what he wore,
Like a badge of love.
Even though the scar on his left cheek
Screamed that he had been to war.

He had seen darkness and cold.
He had tasted the enemy's blood.
He had taken lives in the sadness of wars.
He had cried in the endless fears of many.

But now that is not remembered.
He is no longer a soldier or fighter.
He is no longer the defender of the faith.
He is no longer the protector of the innocent.

Today, wearing his smile,
Just after three o' clock.
In the town square,
Guitar in hand,

He sings his song.
He plays his music.
He moves his soul,
As he moves everyone's soul.

The man with possibly no power,
Stands next to the clock tower.
A reminder to us all:
Be ready for the call.

The Witch's Curse

The witch tried to scare me
With her dark wand.
She cast a spell on me.
'Magic will ruin you,' she said.

'This,' I thought, 'Cannot be true.
Magic is my friend.
My solace, my truth, and my guide.
Magic is gold.'

'No,' she said. 'Magic can turn.
Can make you unlearn.
Can make you unlove.
And can leave you low.'

'This,' I thought, 'Cannot be true.
Magic has always made me glow,
Made me happy and free.
Magic is the warm cool sea.'

'No,' she said. 'Magic is a mystery.
How can a mortal understand this power?
Only the One who rules the hours
Can truly understand this energy.'

'This,' I thought, 'Can be true.
I am a mortal. That is true.
How can I understand why the sky is blue,
Or what lies beyond the morning dew?

'Yes,' she said. 'Magic will ruin you.
So stay away from the light.
Be afraid and stay out of sight.'
This I chant every night.

Like a bolt from the heavens.
The magic light shone bright.
Blinding me, unbinding me… finding me.
Light, light, shining so bright.

When I open to see,
The witch was nowhere
Light all around.
Magic had set me free.

Ether

'Life is a journey,'
Is what the old man said.
Every morning, as you get out of bed,
Remember this in your head.

Play your role as you want to,
Sing your song as you wish to.
Dance in joy, as the angels above
Know that you are pure love.

There may be turns and twists as you proceed.
Have faith that you will always succeed.
With every up there is a down.
Know that you always wear the crown.

Love life as death loves you.
Smile at your enemy.
And know that it is you.
You are the angel and devil, in truth.

Live your soul and take control.
Enjoy the rays of the sun
As it warms your glowing face.
Soon you will disappear without a trace.

Breakfast in Eternity

Lost in the world of my mind
I am searching deep to find ...
Find something that I have not seen for ages.

Something beautiful,
Something pure,
Something magical.

Magic and mystery live within me.
Vibrations of light
Within the matrix of life.

I have known this fact for some time now,
But this mundane life sweeps the magic away.
I would prefer the magic to sweep me away.

Away, far away into the cosmos,
Into my true self,
Into my lucid dreams.

Where I dance with angels,
And breakfast with Gods,
And rest in eternity.

EARTH LIGHT SHINE

1. Freedom
2. The Broken Mirror

Freedom

Free the Earth from her pain.
Wash away her bloodstained face.
Pour love and light to heal …
To heal her deep wounds.

Wounds inflicted by us
Shower her with tears.
Tears of sorrow and regret …
Regret for our inflictions on her.

Show her we will change …
Change to respect her.
Change to love her
Like she loves us.

Like she blesses us.
Let's change to understand and comprehend.
To see and feel in our hands
The grand plan.

Free the Earth from her pain.
Start with a mind release,
Start with a surrender.
Start with yourself.

The Broken Mirror

The golden white bird in the black sky,
The shimmering diamond in the muddy water,
The alchemist who has forgotten his gift …
The world is now in a great paradigm shift.

Mind-altering experiences caused not by drugs,
Mind-altering experiences caused not by alcohol,
Mind-altering experiences caused by shape-shifting creatures…
Creatures with grotesquely beautiful features.

War to bring peace.
Peace to bring war.
Mother Earth lies in agony,
Conquered and concreted by tyranny.

Battered and bruised Mother Earth is.
Scar tissue now holds her together,
Scar tissue that is ready to be ripped apart.
A soul with no heart.

The result is pain to Earth.
Pain to all.
We can prevent this pain.
We need to search within the Earth.

Reach to her core.
Move forward. Walk through the door.
Remove the cataract and see …
See the Earth's crystal.

See the shining light of humanity.
See the hidden truth.
See within.
See …

ETERNAL ECSTASY

1. Another World
2. Stars
3. Halo Infinity
4. One
5. Eternal Ecstasy
6. Existence

Another World

To stand on the moon and see the majestic Earth
Must be really an out-of-this-world experience.

One must feel like Gods and angels gazing at Creation,
Gazing at the beauty - the splendour that is the Earth.

This is the feeling I have …

Every time I gaze into your eyes.
Every time I hear your sweet voice.

Every time I touch you,
And every time you are near.

You are my beautiful Earth.
You are my out-of –this-world experience.

You are …
My supreme heaven on Earth.

You are …
Out of this world.

Stars

Halo, beautiful girl,
Standing here in front of me,
With eyes like shining stars,
And a smile that melts my pain away.

Halo, beautiful girl,
When dark clouds fill my mind,
When fear, doubt, and anger bind,
Your sweet words they heal.

They heal my heart, my mind, my soul.

Halo, beautiful girl,
You are the sun, the stars, the moon.
You are the fire, the earth, the air.
You are the space within my everything.

Halo, beautiful girl,
With your halo shining bright
You make my heart light sing tonight.
Halo, beautiful girl,

Tonight ... make me yours forever.

Halo Infinity

So wonderful looking at you,
Like looking at an angel.

With your halo moving in infinity,
With your wings spreading across the galaxy.

With your radiant all-encompassing glow,
You stand like a shiny star.

Lighting my way home,
Home to your place of love.

With your eternal, magical smile …
With your wings of sweet compassion.

Your song of love.
Your walk of beauty.

You amaze me.
You fulfil me.

You complete me.
You save me.

One

If you believe in love,
If you believe in me,
If you believe in one,
If you believe.

Then what they call time …
This cannot separate us.
Then what they call reality …
This cannot separate us.

If you believe …
That we are one mind,
That we are one heart,
That we are one soul.

In this life, as I lie alone in bed tonight,
I gaze at the pure, white moon.
This white moon, part of a dark night.
I gaze and become connected to your soul.

For whichever galaxy your soul is travelling,
For whichever dimension your heart is residing,
For whichever reality your mind is expanding,
I stay connected …

I stay connected to you,
I live connected to your soul,
I love connected to your heart,
And my thoughts connect to your mind.

No more separation or searching,
As we are one soul.
One soul.
One.

Eternal Ecstasy

As I dance with you under the starlit sky
I gaze into your beautiful eyes,
Your eyes of shimmering heaven.

And what I see simply amazes me.

I see our souls entwined in a dance of love.
I see in you the spirit of my unborn child.
I see in you an eternal, sacred love.

I see in you true reality.

I feel my heart beat with pure love.
I feel a lightness in my soul.
I feel like I have lost all control.

I feel something I have never felt before.

With dancing angels surrounding us
I know that you are my special love.
My amazing, pure-spirited woman.

The reason for my existence.

You, whose smile rivals the sun.
You, whose voice echoes like an angel.
You, who are imbued with the scent of heaven.

And you, whose beauty no other can compare to.

As we continue this spiritual love dance,
Every chamber of my heart fills with light.
Every heartbeat resonates your name.

Eternal ecstasy dwells in my heart.

Existence

The smoky room sins out the existence that I know.
The fire still burns as she dances in the light.
How can one woman create so much passion?
How can one woman be so beautiful?

Seeing her every day,
Watching her, dance, sing, and play,
Gazing into her eyes …
Clearly, I am mesmerized.

Wanting to spend all my time with her,
Wanting never to be alone.
Wanting to wake and sleep in her arms.
The desire to be.

The solar system continues with its evolution.
The world is in a constant revolution.
The light becomes dark.
The left turns to right.

Throughout this era of change,
I remain unchanged.
I stay focused on you,
The reason to be.

A WALK THROUGH MY WORLD

1. A Poet's Solace
2. The Drive
3. Dining With Rats
4. Strings of Heaven
5. Exploration
6. Rented, Unmade Bed
7. True Love Dipped In Blue
8. Juxtaposition
9. Sacred Time
10. The Rescue
11. Internal

A Poet's Solace

A poet writes what is in his mind,
A battling internal discussion.
He is, after all, hoping to find
Some solace from the pain and depression.

Drawing the problems out from his head,
This helps reduce their energy and power.
Sometimes they feel as heavy as lead,
And makes him feel trapped in a tower.

So with the writing a healing takes place,
And the Earth seems still.
A warm glow starts to appear on his face,
And his soul begins to fill.

A feeling complete,
A sight of the divine,
A sensation of pure heat …
Oh, so truly sublime.

He begins to understand the complexities of the sky.
He begins to unravel the mysteries of time.
He feels his wings grow and starts to fly
And knows the time has come for him to shine.

The Drive

I stuff my face with custard creams
And continue to chase my dreams.
Driving up and down the endless road
In search of the highway to my home.

Driving on the road alone,
I pray to God, 'Guide me home.'
Life is dull, tiring, and appears fragmented,
I feel alone, exposed, and unprotected.

Staring at the stars,
I make a wish for love.
Travelling so very far,
I continue asking for guidance from above.

Is the lesson patience?
Is the lesson faith?
Is the lesson confidence?
Or am I too late?

Angels in heaven, shine your light on me.
Angels of purpose, show your face.
Angels of love, set me free.
Angels of patience, curb my haste.

Dining With Rats

Give up the sugars, give up the fats,
Give up smoking, give up dining with rats,
Give up drinking from the sewer,
And then maybe you can cure her.

Her playful and lustful ways are set to capture you,
Appearing as innocent and sweet as morning dew.
Those fiery eyes set in her mysterious face
Leaves you with only pity and disgrace.

She transports your mind to another dimension.
She relaxes your body in sweet submission.
Your dreams are that of infinite creations,
But the very next moment you have no recollections.

And when you return back to Planet Earth,
Back to your existence of dull and grey,
You start to count from one to ten,
For part of you knows you have lost the way.

There is no good to come of this alliance,
Only more karmic debt to add.
So abandon this strong reliance,
Or else you will most truly go mad.

Strings of Heaven

I am in search of God,
But I keep meeting the devil.
I left home and travelled abroad,
But the dark lord still meddles.

I am in search of love and a home,
But I keep existing in a house alone.
I have travelled so long. I now live in sorrow.
My life still seems dull and narrow.

I am in search of rebirth,
And wish to grow golden wings.
I have smelt the foulness of death,
And heard my bright soul sing.

I have indulged in pleasure and sin.
I have intoxicated my body and mind.
I start to strum my guitar so I can begin ...
Begin to understand, search and to find.

I have travelled twice to India and met God.
On my second visit God took him away.
I prayed and prayed to the Lord,
'Please allow him to stay.'

God's will, will always prevail. We have to abide.
And when he breathed his last breath
I was happy to be by his side,
To be comforted by family in this time of death.

I was alone, lost in grief and pity.
I was alone in the dark and cold.
God sent divine angels to heal me.
I began to realise that I was not in control.

I surrender to Him.
I pray to Him.
God's will, will prevail.
I have to abide.

Exploration

Where is my heart?
It feels ripped apart
With tired and torn muscles
Due to life's hustle, life's bustle.

I take no rest,
I take no sleep.
Because to rest with sleep
Is a time to think.

A time to think …
To think about my isolation on this island
Away from home, love, and family.
Away from reality.

A self-induced prison.
A self-imposed cage.
A cage of growth.
And a prison of freedom.

A necessary part of the journey,
A journey of understanding,
A journey of creativity,
A journey of truth.

A difficult, loving, and healing exploration.
An exploration, a journey, a story
Deep into the depth and mystery of my…
Creative soul.

Rented, Unmade Bed

The black and broken tree,
The rented, unmade bed.
The sweet nightingale is free,
But the pain is still in my head.

The unironed white shirt,
The untidy bedroom.
The silver car with layers of dirt,
And my face full of gloom.

A cupboard full of important papers,
A home I do not own.
My search for the maker,
And…my unpaid loan.

My unshaven face of grey,
My tired and worn-out face.
Days turn to night and night to day,
Please, Lord, I humbly ask for your grace.

My quest for eternity
In a job that frustrates.
Should I go back to university?
Or simply just accept my fate.

A question to the universe…
Am I alive or dead?
As it seems my mind is in reverse
Maybe I should just… make my bed.

True Love Dipped In Blue

She told me that she loves him.
She told me that he is everything.
She told me that he loves her,
But for now they stay apart.

Apart they stay,
Scared to get to the heart.
Happy to remain apart,
Yet so close they remain.

I will not understand this.
Maybe it's their karma.
I urged her to end this drama,
And live in bliss.

What can I do?
It hurts to see true love dipped in blue.
All light is bright.
I am sure He will see them through.

Juxtaposition

Seconds to minutes,
Minutes to hours,
Hours to days.

Days to years,
Years to tears,
Tears to fears.

To play this drama,
To endure this trauma.
Is this my karma?

Spiritual light shines bright...

Spiritual light juxtaposed with mental anarchy.
Universal understanding juxtaposed
With worldly ignorance.

A hero to save the world,
Or a zero in search of a girl?
My mind caught in a twirl.

Mortal man
Or divine being?
Who am I?

Sacred Time

I lay awake at night, unable to sleep.
Insomnia is a curse.
My mind is jumping leaps and leaps.
Insomnia is a curse.

I do try my very best,
But a peaceful sleep I cannot find.
I cannot lay my heavy head to rest.
I cannot close my eyes or my mind.

I cannot rest throughout the night,
Although my dream world awaits me.
I cannot enter this luxury and light.
I remain trapped in this wakeful insanity.

My passage that is sleep
Has been taken away.
I am forced to remain in the mundane.
To the angels of serenity and sleep I do pray.

I need to sleep to regain my sanity.
I need to sleep to regain my soul.
I need to rest, not merely for vanity.
I need to rest to remain in control.

Dear angels of serenity and sleep,
Shower your sacred angel dust,
As I cannot continue counting sheep.
Sleep tonight, I pray. I must.

Make me rest, make me retreat,
Into the beauty that is sleep.
With your power, this should be an easy feat,
Make me sleep, make me sleep, make me sleep.

The Rescue

I light my cigarette
To burn my soul,
To punish my lungs.

I cough the phlegm of discontent.
I bring on cancer.
I am the hapless chancer.

I believe in God,
I believe in angels,
I believe in love.

I feel the pain. Is there something to gain?
I am surrounded by cigarette smoke.
Reality is what I do not believe in.

Trapped in this grey illusion,
Seeing truth only in dreams,
Seeing angels dancing in the sky.

Hearing the sweet music of heaven,
Searching for bliss,
Trying to rescue my soul.

Trying to get back control,
I extinguish my cigarette.
And my life begins.

Internal

I know love exists.
I know God exists.
I know truth exists.

So why do I continue to resist?
Why do I continue to protest?
Why do I continue to persist?

Persist to walk away,
And sometimes run away.
Run away.

Run away from love,
Run away from God,
And from the truth.

Is the pull of pleasure that strong?
That it will take me to a place
Where I know I do not belong.

Is the need for defiance
And the lack of compliance
An attack by the mind on the soul?

An internal fight
To see who is in control…
The mind or the soul?

The battle continues…

CHALLENGE FOR CHANGE

1. Divine Wealth
2. Only God Knows
3. Treasured Gold
4. The Fallen's Immortality

Divine Wealth

East and west, both trying to be the best,
While suffering is bestowed upon the rest.
Wars have been fought, wars are being fought, wars will be fought.
We have not learnt what the teachers have taught.

Because of our greed and power-filled souls,
We have lost all sense of control.
Sacrificed at the altar of golden materialistic divinity,
We pray at her diamond-embedded platinum feet.

Throwing all the wealth we have
And all the wealth we do not have
At her sacred sole,
We indebt ourselves to her and nestle deep within her.

An ecstatic union of supreme superficiality.

Is there a way to reverse?
Have we got time to pause?
Is there a way out?
Do we even know the way out?

The way out is…

In.

Only God Knows

See the stars shine so bright.
See the moonlight shining through.
The heavenly night is such a beautiful sight.
All is restful. All is calm.

All the people are asleep,
But what will the dawn bring?
As the angels now do not sing…
Their celestial flight has now ceased.

As man's soul starts to freeze
The beast is free, roaming with fire.
The anger surges, as do sweet desires,
Beastly desires raging with infinite heat.

East and west are at war,
So many times this battle fought before.
Only God knows of the true score,
Only God knows.

We fight for oil, land, and power,
We even believe we fight for God.
While every minute and every hour,
The beast grows within to extreme power.

How can we destroy the beast?
How can we stop the pain?
First realise there is nothing to gain.
All that we seek is within.

All that we need is in our heart.
All that we need is faith.
All that we need is love.
Love is all we need.

Treasured Gold

The drums of war are once again beating.
Beating faster and louder.
Stand up. Fight against.
Defend your truth.

The calls for peace are deafened.
Everyone now wants a piece,
A piece of this treasured gold.
At the risk of losing all control.

The drums of war are now beating louder.
The people have risen.
Defending their truth.
Fighting against.

The heavenly trumpets continue their call
As they have always done.
The angels continue their flight.
Celestial lights shining bright.

The calls for peace still echo
Through the war-ravaged land.
The people now question their truth.
A truth they have defended…and befriended.

The treasured gold that they hold
Is nothing more than misguided truth.
Is nothing more than false ideology.
Is nothing more than untrue prophesy.

As the people sit down to ponder
And reflect with regret.
They search for answers
Only to find more questions.

The Fallen's Immortality*

Like a river of blood
Flowing around the tower,
A reminder to us all: Forget about the power.
Forget about the power.

Like a river of hearts
Around the tower bleeding,
A reminder to us all: Forget about the greed.
Forget about the greed.

Like the souls of many
Lost forever across the land,
A reminder to us all: Love your fellow man.
Love your fellow man.

Millions of poppies in ceramic
Reflecting the many that bled,
Reflecting the tear in the fabric
In a society ripped and gripped by war.

A hundred years have gone
Since the Great War begun.
As the new dawn begins
We pray that it will bring.

Bring us to the light.
Bring us forward.
Bring us peace.
Bring us some…release.

So a time to remember and reflect,
A time not to forget
The heroes that have fallen,
But have risen to immortality.

Like a river of love
Flowing around the tower,
A reminder to us all: Love is all we need.
Love is all we need.

Written after visiting the ceramic poppy display around the Tower of London, 2014

ONE TRUE LIGHT

1. Vibrations
2. Lucid Mind
3. Unborn
4. Echoes of Light
5. Perfect
6. The Return

Vibrations

As I look into the night sky
Shining stars like beautiful eyes
Gaze lovingly back at me
…I feel free!

A feeling of mysterious release,
A moment of peace.
A connection between the cosmos and me
Felt so deep, I can only weep.

My mind is free from these chains.
My heart feels no more pain.
My soul vibrates with energy.
I can now hear the angel's symphony.

My heart shines so bright,
A truly beautiful sight.
A feeling of pure love,
To be at one with all that is above.

Lucid Mind

One single stream of the lucid mind,
One continuous thought,
One ideology,
One frequency.

Tune yourself to it.
Feel the difference of being one,
Feel the joy and bliss,
Feel the formless.

See the divine form,
See the supreme beauty,
See with the inner eye,
See the oneness.

Breathe the air of oneness,
Gaze at the everlasting truth,
See the divine form, feel the formless,
Tune into your heart.

The journey of the soul…the voyage of the heart.
This is the oneness of all humanity,
The oneness of all creation,
The oneness of the mind.

Oneness of the heart,
One heart of all, vibrating with love.
One single stream of pure love,
One single stream of the lucid mind.

Unborn

She downs another tequila,
Smokes another cigarette,
And then she reflects…
Has God forgotten her?

She smokes to burn her soul.
She drinks to lose control.
She lives in dark regret.
Has God forgotten her?

She knows new life grows within.
She knows she abuses the embryo of new.
She tries hard to forget.
Has God forgotten her?

Is new birth the door to death?
Is new birth the passage to life?
She again reflects.
Has God *really* forgotten her?

Maybe this is her second chance.
A chance to give what she never got
A light sign from deep within,
That He has not forgot.

This growth, this life, this soul.
The one that she can mould.
The one she will shelter from the cold.
She knows she has to hand over control.

He has not forgot.
He has always been there by her side.
For in her He resides,
As He resides in the life within her.

This very small ray.
This tiny fragment of a soul.
A cell within the whole.
A smiling light to a new day.

She extinguishes the cigarette.
Breaks the bottle with no regret.
Smiles a beam of light.
And places her hand on this new life.

He has *never* forgot.
It is she that has forgot.
He has always been by her side.
In her is where He resides.

Echoes of Light

Have you ever heard an angel's voice?
I hope and pray you get the chance.
To hear pure love speak
Fills your soul with inner peace.

Words of truth that will set you free.
Words of love that will make you see.
Your mind is free from the prison chains.
No more suffering and no more pain.

Your soul is alive with God's energy,
And you now hear the angel's symphony.
Have you ever heard an angel's voice?
I hope and pray you get the chance.

All your troubles start to fade away,
Tomorrow you know will be a better day.
Angels dry away all your tears.
Angels smile away all your fears.

They make you see through the illusion.
And rescue your mind from confusion.
You are awoken by the sweet angel sound,
And have a feeling that you have just been found.

You look around for the light beams.
For nothing is as it seems
And then you think…
Has this been but a dream?

Perfect

As the delicate butterfly flaps its wings,
And the heavenly birds start to sing,
As the bees create their honey,
And the sun spreads his light

On all of God's creatures.

I feel blessed to be part
Of this beautiful Earth.
An Earth full of love, light, and peace.
An Earth full of hope, joy, and promise.

So wonderful it is to be alive.

Thank you, God.
Thank you, Lord.
Thank you for your perfect creations.
Perfect is creation.

The Return

Think of life,
Think of death,
Think of every person that you've ever met.

Think of the stars,
Think of the earth,
Think of the blood pumping in your heart.

Think of the ocean,
Think of the blue sky,
Think of the flight of the pure white dove.

Think of purity,
Think of unity,
Think of divinity.

Think of human essence,
Think of divine presence.
Where does it all begin?

When the soul starts to sing,
When the joy that you bring,
Enhances every living thing.

Then the mission of this birth,
Will complete its journey,
And return to the light.

Until We Meet Again...

As you move forward in your journey...

May the angels be your guide,
May the light be your shadow,
May the truth be your protector,
And may faith be your healer.

Peace, Peace, Peace...

About The Poet

Manivasagan (Mani) is a poet who was born in Durban, South Africa, where he trained as a Physiotherapist. At the age of 25 he relocated to the United Kingdom to continue his career, and is still working as a Physiotherapist in the UK.

At a young age, Mani, loved poetry and music and at school really enjoyed the 'creative writing' classes.

His first poem, 'Rhythmical Energy Beams' was written in London in April, 2004 and thereafter, like magic, his craft flowed beautifully.

His influences include poets like Mathew Arnold, Sylvia Platt and Williams Wordsworth. He remembers reading Mathew Arnold's 'Dover Beach', Sylvia Platt's, 'Mushrooms' and William Wordsworth's 'Daffodils' and being amazed at the power and beauty of words.

He is also greatly influenced by singer songwriters like John Lennon and Paul McCartney of the Beatles, Bob Marley and James Blunt. He finds that these 'poets' create a musical background to their craft that takes the listener to another world.

A writer, Mani really admires is Paulo Coehlo and one of his favourite books is the 'The Alchemist'. He finds that this book has much depth and energy, and that the story is told with real beauty.

His other interest is abstract artwork and he has been painting for the last ten years. The cover of this poetry book, 'Mystical

Lights' was painted by Mani using acrylic paint. He loves the richness and texture of this medium and finds painting another way for him to express himself.